Psalms of Solomon

By

King Solomon

Copyright © 2020 Lamp of Trismegistus. All rights reserved. No part of this publication may be reproduced or transmitted in any form or by any means, electronic or mechanical, including photocopying, recording, or by any information storage and retrieval system, without permission in writing from Lamp of Trismegistus. Reviewers may quote brief passages.

ISBN: 978-1-63118-439-0

Christian Apocrypha Series

Other Books in this Series and Related Titles

The Testament of Abraham by Abraham (978-1-63118-441-3)

The Book of Astronomical Secrets by Enoch (978-1-63118-443-7)

Book of Dreams by Enoch (978-1-63118-437-6)

The Lives of Adam and Eve by Moses (978-1-63118-414-7)

The First and Second Gospels of the Infancy of Jesus Christ by Thomas and James (978-1-63118-415-4)

Lost Chapters of the Book of Daniel and Related Writings by Daniel (978-1-63118-417-8)

The Testament of Moses by Moses (978-1-63118-440-6)

The Book of the Watchers by Enoch (978-1-63118-416-1)

The Book of Parables by Enoch (978-1-63118-429-1)

Masonic Symbolism of Easter and the Christ in Masonry by various authors (978-1-63118-434-5)

A Few Masonic Sermons by A. C. Ward & Bascom B. Clarke (978-1-63118-435-2)

Masonic Symbolism of King Solomon's Temple by Albert G. Mackey & others (978-1-63118-442-0)

Cloud Upon the Sanctuary by A. E. Waite & K. Eckartshausen (978-1-63118-438-3)

The Two Great Pillars of Boaz and Jachin by Albert G. Mackey & others (978-1-63118-433-8)

Audio Versions are also Available on Audible and iTunes

Table of Contents

Introduction…7

Preface…9

Original Prologue…13

Psalm I…15

Psalm II…17

Psalm III…21

Psalm IV…23

Psalm V…27

Psalm VI…29

Psalm VII…31

Psalm VIII…33

Psalm IX…37

Psalm X…39

Psalm XI…41

Psalm XII…43

Psalm XIII…45

Psalm XIV…47

Psalm XV…49

Psalm XVI…51

Psalm XVII…53

Psalm XVIII…59

Introduction

The Apocrypha are a loosely knit series of books, written by early vanguards of Christianity (covering the eras of both the old and new testaments), and which comprise somewhere between about a dozen to several hundred titles, depending on whom you ask and how that person defines "Apocrypha." A small selection of these can still be found included in the Catholic bible, while a majority of the books in question, were abandoned by church officials in the early centuries of Christianity. Many of these apocryphal books were originally considered canon by early followers of Christ, in the first four centuries following his birth. It wasn't until the meeting of the Council of Nicaea in 325, that Emperor Constantine and a group of roughly 300 church bishops, gathered together with the goal of defining, standardizing and unifying an otherwise splintering Christianity, that many of these writings ceased to be included in the newly established canon. Enjoy then, this book as an example, of just one of the many books of the Christian Apocrypha, and be sure to check out other titles in this series.

Preface

Just for good measure, let's brush up on a bit of history as well as review a few of the basics, before diving into this collection. For starters, some of you might be wondering about the word "psalm" itself, while others might be asking themselves about Solomon, while still others are remembering that psalms are more usually associated with David, rather than Solomon.

So, what is a psalm; what does the word actually mean? Simply put, a psalm is a sacred song, hymn or a lyrical poem used for the praise or worship of God, often intended to be set to musical accompaniment.

Generally, when we hear the word "psalm," we tend to think of the traditional 150 psalms that collectively comprise the *Book of Psalms* of the Old Testament. Of these 150 psalms, about half of them are traditionally attributed to David.

King David has a historical reputation as being an early example of a Renaissance Man, one might say. David's earliest claim to fame, during his youth, was that of being a renowned and beloved musician, whose many songs would find a future home among the numerous odes he authored, in the *Book of Psalms*. While still a young shepherd, he became further esteemed by the masses when he slayed the giant known as Goliath. From there, he would go on to be anointed as king, conquer Jerusalem and ultimately build a reputation as the ideal king, before appointing his son, Solomon, as his successor to the throne.

David, as we have already established, is author of the lion's share of the *Book of Psalms*, but what of the rest of the book? In that regard, about a third of the psalms are unattributed, while the remainder have their attribution of authorship spread between six historical individuals. Of those six people, one of them is, in fact, King Solomon, who is attributed to having written two of the Psalms; specifically, numbers 72 and 127. Of these, Psalm 72 is generally considered to be more notable and truer to the voice of Solomon. Here is Psalm 72, as a comparison to keep in mind, while you are reading the further 18 *Psalms of Solomon* which are to come:

> *Endow the king with your justice, O God,*
> > *the royal son with your righteousness.*
>
> *May he judge your people in righteousness,*
> > *your afflicted ones with justice.*
>
> *May the mountains bring prosperity to the people,*
> > *the hills the fruit of righteousness.*
>
> *May he defend the afflicted among the people*
> > *and save the children of the needy;*
> > *may he crush the oppressor.*
>
> *May he endure as long as the sun,*
> > *as long as the moon, through all generations.*
>
> *May he be like rain falling on a mown field,*
> > *like showers watering the earth.*
>
> *In his days may the righteous flourish*
> > *and prosperity abound till the moon is no more.*
>
> *May he rule from sea to sea*
> > *and from the River to the ends of the earth.*
>
> *May the desert tribes bow before him*
> > *and his enemies lick the dust.*

May the kings of Tarshish and of distant shores
    bring tribute to him.
May the kings of Sheba and Seba
    present him gifts.
May all kings bow down to him
    and all nations serve him.
For he will deliver the needy who cry out,
    the afflicted who have no one to help.
He will take pity on the weak and the needy
    and save the needy from death.
He will rescue them from oppression and violence,
    for precious is their blood in his sight.
Long may he live!
    May gold from Sheba be given him.
May people ever pray for him
    and bless him all day long.
May grain abound throughout the land;
    on the tops of the hills may it sway.
May the crops flourish like Lebanon
    and thrive like the grass of the field.
May his name endure forever;
    may it continue as long as the sun.
Then all nations will be blessed through him,
    and they will call him blessed.
Praise be to the Lord God, the God of Israel,
    who alone does marvelous deeds.
Praise be to his glorious name forever;
    may the whole earth be filled with his glory.
Amen and Amen.

King Solomon is traditionally known for a number of things, among those for being the builder of the first temple of Jerusalem. He was also widely recognized as being exceedingly wise.

His renowned wisdom came to him as a gift from God. Following a sacrifice, God appeared to Solomon in a dream, asking Solomon what he most desired. Solomon responded by asking God to grant him wisdom. God was pleased that Solomon didn't ask for something self-serving and consequently, chose to grant his reward. As a result, the name of King Solomon is usually synonymous with the attribute of great wisdom. Perhaps the most familiar tale demonstrating his wisdom is a story known as the Judgement of Solomon. In this story, two women each lay a claim to the same child. Solomon ordered the child be cut in half and each woman given one half of the child. This resulted in one woman renouncing her claim of motherhood, in order to spare the child from death. Solomon wisely realized that the woman who was willing to sacrifice her claim on the child in order to save it, must be the true mother.

Solomon is also remembered for being the prolific author of numerous biblical books: *Proverbs*, *Ecclesiastes*, *Song of Songs* and *Wisdom of Solomon*, as well as this one.

Presented here, then, are the 18 psalms that make up the apocryphal book, the *Psalms of Solomon*, just as they were first published in English, along with the original prologue.

Original Prologue

This collection of eighteen war songs are the gift of an ancient Semitic writer. The original manuscript has perished but fortunately Greek translations have been preserved, and a Syriac version of the same songs has turned up and was published in English for the first time in 1909, by Dr. Rendel Harris.

The date of the writing may be established at the middle of the First Century B. C. because the theme of these songs is that of Pompey's actions in Palestine and his death in Egypt in 48 B. C.

These psalms had an important position and were widely circulated in the early Church. They are frequently referred to in the various Codexes and histories of the first few centuries of the Christian Era.

Later, they became lost through inexplicable reasons; and have only been recovered for our use after the lapse of many centuries.

Besides the literary value of the trumpet-like rhythm of these verses, we have here a chapter of stirring ancient history written by an eyewitness. Pompey comes out of the West. He uses battering- rams on the fortifications. His soldiers defile the altar. He is slain in Egypt after a fearful career. In the "righteous" of these psalms we see the Pharisees; in the "sinners" we see the Sadducees. It is an epic of a great people in the throes of a great crisis.

Psalm I

"They became insolent in their prosperity..."

I cried unto the Lord when I was in distress,
>   Unto God when sinners assailed.

Suddenly the alarm of war was heard before me;
>   I said, He will hearken to me for I am full of righteousness.

I thought in my heart that I was full of righteousness,
>   Because I was well off and had become rich in children.

Their wealth spread to the whole earth,
>   And their glory unto the end of the earth.

They were exalted unto the stars;
>   They said they would never fall.

But they became insolent in their prosperity,
>   And they were without understanding,

Their sins were in secret,
>   And even I had no knowledge of them.

Their transgressions went beyond those of the heathen before them;
>   They utterly polluted the holy things of the Lord.

Psalm II

The desecration of Jerusalem; captivity, murder, and raping. A psalm of utter despair.

When the sinner waxed proud, with a battering-ram he cast down fortified walls,
    And thou didst not restrain him.
Alien nations ascended Thine altar,
    They trampled it proudly with their sandals;
Because the sons of Jerusalem had defiled the holy things of the Lord,
    Had profaned with iniquities the offerings of God.
Therefore He said: Cast them far from Me;

It was set at naught before God,
    It was utterly dishonored;
The sons and the daughters were in grievous captivity,
    Sealed was their neck, branded was it among the nations.

According to their sins hath He done unto them,
    For He hath left them in the hands of them that prevailed.
He hath turned away His face from pitying them,
    Young and old and their children together;
For they had done evil one and all, in not hearkening.
    And the heavens were angry,
And the earth abhorred them;
    For no man upon it had done what they did,
And the earth recognized all
    Thy righteous judgments, O God.

They set the sons of Jerusalem to be mocked at in return for
the harlots in her;
> Every wayfarer entered in in the full light of day.

They made mock with their transgressions, as they themselves
were wont to do;
> In the full light of day they revealed their iniquities.

And the daughters of Jerusalem were defiled in accordance
with Thy judgment,
> Because they had defiled themselves with unnatural
> intercourse.

I am pained in my bowels and my inward parts for these
things.

And yet I will justify Thee, O God, in uprightness of heart,
For in Thy judgments is Thy righteousness displayed, O
> God.

For Thou hast rendered to the sinners according to their
deeds,
> Yea, according to their sins, which were very wicked.

Thou hast uncovered their sins, that Thy judgment might be
manifest;
> Thou hast wiped out their memorial from the earth.

God is a righteous judge,
> And he is no respecter of persons.

For the nations reproached Jerusalem, trampling it down;
> Her beauty was dragged down from the throne of glory.

She girded on sackcloth instead of comely raiment,
> A rope was about her head instead of a crown.

She put off the glorious diadem which God had set upon her,

    In dishonor was her beauty cast upon the ground.

And I saw and entreated the Lord and said,
    Long enough, O Lord has Thine hand been heavy on
Israel, in bringing the nations upon them.
For they have made sport unsparingly in wrath and fierce
anger;
    And they will make an utter end, unless Thou, O Lord,
rebuke them in Thy wrath.
For they have done. it not in zeal, but in lust of soul,
    Pouring out their wrath upon us with a view to rapine.
Delay not, O God, to recompense them on their heads,
    To turn the pride of the dragon into dishonor.
And I had not long to wait before God showed me the
insolent one
    Slain on the mountains of Egypt,
    Esteemed of less account than the least, on land and sea;
His body, too, borne hither and thither on the billows with
much insolence,
    With none to bury him, because He had rejected him with
dishonor.

He reflected not that he was man,
    And reflected not on the latter end;
He said: I will be lord of land and sea;

And he recognized not that it is God who is great,
    Mighty in His great strength.
He is king over the heavens,
    And judgeth kings and kingdoms.
It is He who setteth me up in glory,
    And bringeth down the proud to eternal destruction in dishonor,
    Because they knew Him not.

And now behold, ye princes of the earth, the judgement of the Lord,
    For a great king and righteous is He, judging all that is under heaven.
Bless God, ye that fear the Lord with wisdom,
    For the mercy of the Lord will be upon them that fear Him, in the Judgement;
So that He will distinguish between the righteous and the
    sinner,
And recompense the sinners for ever according to their deeds;

And have mercy on the righteous, delivering him from the affliction of the sinner,
    And recompensing the sinner for what he hath done to the righteous.
For the Lord is good to them that call upon Him in patience,

    Doing according to His mercy to His pious ones,
    Establishing them at all times before Him in strength.

Blessed be the Lord for ever before His servants.

Psalm III

Righteousness versus Sin.

Why sleepest thou, O my soul,
    And blessest not the Lord?
Sing a new song,
    Unto God who is worthy to be praised.
Sing and be wakeful against His awaking,
    For good is a psalm sung to God from a glad heart.

The righteous remember the Lord at all times,
    With thanksgiving and declaration of the righteousness of the Lord's judgements.
The righteous despiseth not the chastening of the Lord;
    His will is always before the Lord.
The righteous stumbleth and holdeth the Lord righteous:
    He falleth and looketh out for what God will do to him;
He seeketh out whence his deliverance will come.
    The steadfastness of the righteous is from God, their deliverer;
There lodgeth not in the house of the righteous sin upon sin.

    The righteous continually searcheth his house,
To remove utterly all iniquity done by him in error.
    He maketh atonement for sins of ignorance by fasting and afflicting his soul,
And the Lord counteth guiltless every pious man and his house.

The sinner stumbleth and curseth his life
The day when he was begotten, and his mother's travail.
He addeth sins to sins, while he liveth;
He falleth--verily grievous is his fall--and riseth no more.
The destruction of the sinner is for ever,
And he shall not be remembered, when the righteous is visited.
This is the portion of sinners for ever.

But they that fear the Lord shall rise to life eternal,
And their life shall be in the light of the Lord, and shall come to an end no more.

Psalm IV

A conversation of Solomon with the Men-pleasers.

Wherefore sittest thou, O profane man, in the council of the pious,

> Seeing that thy heart is far removed from the Lord,
> Provoking with transgressions the God of Israel?

Extravagant in speech, extravagant in outward seeming beyond all men,

> Is he that is severe of speech in condemning sinners in judgement.

And his hand is first upon him as though he acted in zeal,

> And yet he is himself guilty in respect of manifold sins and of wantonness.

His eyes are upon every woman without distinction;

> His tongue lieth when he maketh contract with an oath.

By night and in secret he sinneth as though unseen,

> With his eyes he talketh to every woman of evil compacts.

He is swift to enter every house with cheerfulness as though guileless.
Let God remove those that live in hypocrisy in the company of the pious,

> Even the life of such an one with corruption of his flesh and penury.

Let God reveal the deeds of the men-pleasers,

> The deeds of such an one with laughter and derision;

That the pious may count righteous the judgement of their God,
> When sinners are removed from before the righteous,
> Even the man-pleaser who uttereth law guilefully.

And their eyes are fixed upon any man's house that is still secure,
> That they may, like the Serpent, destroy the wisdom of... with words of transgressors,

His words are deceitful that he may accomplish his wicked desire.
> He never ceaseth from scattering families as though they were orphans,
> Yea, he layeth waste a house on account of his lawless desire.

He deceiveth with words, saying, There is none that seeth, or judgeth.
He fills one house with lawlessness,
> And then his eyes are fixed upon the next house,
> To destroy it with words that give wing to desire.

Yet with all these his soul like Sheol, is not sated.

Let his portion, O Lord, be dishonoured before thee;
> Let him go forth groaning, and come home cursed.

Let his life be spent in anguish, and penury, and want, O Lord;
> Let his sleep be beset with pains and his awaking with perplexities.

Let sleep be withdrawn from his eyelids at night;

> Let him fail dishonourably in every work of his hands.

Let him come home empty-handed to his house,

> And his house be void of everything wherewith he could

sate his appetite.

Let his old age be spent in childless loneliness until his

removal by death.

Let the flesh of the men-pleasers be rent by wild beasts,

> And let the bones of the lawless lie dishonoured in the

sight of the sun.

Let ravens peck out the eyes of the hypocrites.

For they have laid waste many houses of men, in dishonour,

> And scattered them in their lust;

And they have not remembered God,

> Nor feared God in all these things;

> But they have provoked God's anger and vexed Him.

May He remove them from off the earth,

> Because with deceit they beguiled the souls of the

flawless.

Blessed are they that fear the Lord in their flawlessness;

> The Lord shall deliver them from guileful men and

sinners,

> And deliver us from every stumbling-block of the lawless

(men).

Let God destroy them that insolently work all

unrighteousness,

> For a great and mighty judge is the Lord our God in
> righteousness.

Let Thy mercy, O Lord, be upon all them that love Thee.

Psalm V

A statement of the philosophy of the indestructibility of matter. One of the tenets of modern physics.

O Lord God, I will praise Thy name with joy,
    In the midst of them that know Thy righteous judgements.
For Thou art good and merciful, the refuge of the poor;
    When I cry to Thee, do not silently disregard me.
For no man taketh spoil from a mighty man;
    Who, then, can take aught of a that Thou hast made, except Thou Thyself givest?
For man and his portion lie before Thee in the balance;
    He cannot add to, so as to enlarge, what has been prescribed by Thee.

O God, when we are in distress we call upon Thee for help,
    And Thou dost not turn back our petition, for Thou art our God.
Cause not Thy hand to be heavy upon us,
    Lest through necessity we sin.
Even though Thou restore us not, we will not keep away;
    But unto Thee will we come.
For if I hunger, unto Thee will I cry, O God;
    And *Thou* wilt give to me.

Birds and fish dost Thou nourish,
    In that Thou givest rain to the steppes that green grass

may spring up,
    So to prepare fodder in the steppe for every living thing;
And if they hunger, unto Thee do they lift up their face.
Kings and rulers and peoples Thou dost nourish, O God;
    And who is the help of the poor and needy, if not Thou, O Lord?
And Thou wilt hearken--for who is good and gentle but thou?--
    Making glad the soul of the humble by opening Thine hand in mercy.

Man's goodness is bestowed grudgingly and ...;
    And if he repeat it without murmuring, even that is marvelous.
But Thy gift is great in goodness and wealth,
    And he whose hope is set on Thee shall have no lack of gifts.
Upon the whole earth is Thy mercy, O Lord, in goodness.
Happy is he whom God remembereth in granting to him a due sufficiency;
    If a man abound overmuch, he sinneth.
Sufficient are moderate means with righteousness,
    And hereby the blessing of the Lord becomes abundance with righteousness.
They that fear the Lord rejoice in good gifts,
    And thy goodness is upon Israel in Thy kingdom.
Blessed is the glory of the Lord, for He is our king.

Psalm VI

A song of hope and fearlessness and peace.

Happy is the man whose heart is fixed to call upon the name of the Lord;
    When he remembereth the name of the Lord, he will be saved.
His ways are made even by the Lord,
    And the works of his hands are preserved by the Lord his God.
At what he sees in his bad dreams, his soul shall not be troubled;
    When he passes through rivers and the tossing of the seas, he shall not be dismayed.
He ariseth from his sleep, and blesseth the name of the Lord:
    When his heart is at peace, he singeth to the name of his God,
    And he entreateth the Lord for all his house.
And the Lord heareth the prayer of every one that feareth God,
    And every request of the soul that hopes for Him doth the Lord accomplish.

Blessed is the Lord, who showeth mercy to those who love Him in sincerity.

Psalm VII

The fine old doctrine--"Thou art our Shield!"

Make not Thy dwelling afar from us, O God;
  Lest they assail us that hate us without cause.
For Thou hast rejected them, O God;
    Let not their foot trample upon Thy holy inheritance.
Chasten us Thyself in Thy good pleasure;
  But give us not up to the nations;
For, if Thou sendest pestilence,
  Thou Thyself givest it charge concerning us;
For Thou art merciful,
    And wilt not be angry to the point of consuming us.

While Thy name dwelleth in our midst, we shall find mercy;
  And the nations shall not prevail against us.
For Thou art our shield,
  And when we call upon Thee, Thou hearkenest to us;
For Thou wilt pity the seed of Israel for ever
  And Thou wilt not reject them:
But we shall, be under Thy yoke for ever,
  And under the rod of Thy chastening.
Thou wilt establish us in the time that Thou helpest us,
  Showing mercy to the house of Jacob on the day wherein
Thou didst promise to help them.

Psalm VIII

Some remarkable similes of war creeping on Jerusalem. A survey of the sins that brought all this trouble.

Distress and the sound of war hath my ear heard,
> The sound of a trumpet announcing slaughter and calamity,

The sound of much people as of an exceeding high wind,
> As a tempest with mighty fire sweeping through the Negeb.

And I said in my heart, Surely God judgeth us;
> A sound I hear moving towards Jerusalem, the holy city

My loins were broken at what I heard, my knees tottered;
> My heart was afraid, my bones were dismayed like flax.

I said: They establish their ways in righteousness.

I thought upon the judgments of God since the creation of heaven and earth;
> I held God righteous in His judgements which have been from of old.

God bare their sins in the full light of day;
> All the earth came to know the righteous judgements of God.

In secret places underground their iniquities were committed to provoke Him to anger;
They wrought confusion, son with mother and father with
> daughter;

They committed adultery, every man with his neighbour's wife.

They concluded covenants with one another with an oath touching these things;

They plundered the sanctuary of God, as though there was no avenger.

They trode the altar of the Lord, coming straight from all manner of uncleanness;

And with menstrual blood they defiled the sacrifices, as though these were common flesh.

They left no sin undone, wherein they surpassed not the heathen.

Therefore God mingled for them a spirit of wandering;

And gave them to drink a cup of undiluted wine, that they might become drunken.

He brought him that is from the end of the earth, that smiteth mightily;

He decreed war against Jerusalem, and against her land. The princes of the land went to meet him with joy: they said unto him:

Blessed be thy way! Come ye, enter ye in with peace.

They made the rough ways even, before his entering in;

They opened the gates to Jerusalem, they crowned its walls.

As a father entereth the house of his sons, so he entered Jerusalem in peace;

He established his feet there in great safety.

He captured her fortresses and the wall of Jerusalem;

    For God Himself led him in safety, while they wandered.

He destroyed their princes and every one wise in counsel;

    He poured out the blood of the inhabitants of Jerusalem, like the water of uncleanness.

He led away their sons and daughters, whom they had begotten in defilement.

They did according to their uncleanness, even as their fathers had done:

    They defiled Jerusalem and the things that had been hallowed to the name of God.

But God hath shown Himself righteous in His judgements upon the nations of the earth;

    And the pious servants of God are like innocent lambs in their midst.

Worthy to be praised is the Lord that judgeth the whole earth in His righteousness.

Behold, now, O God, Thou hast shown us Thy judgement in Thy righteousness;

    Our eyes have seen Thy judgements, O God.

We have justified Thy name that is honoured for ever;

    For Thou are the God of righteousness, judging Israel with chastening.

Turn, O God, Thy mercy upon us, and have pity upon us;

    Gather together the dispersed of Israel, with mercy and

goodness;

For Thy faithfulness is with us,

And though we have stiffened our neck, yet Thou art our chastener;

    Overlook us not, O our God, lest the nations swallow us up, as though there were none to deliver.

But Thou art our God from the beginning,

    And upon Thee is our hope set, O Lord;

And we will not depart from Thee,

    For good are Thy judgements upon us.

Ours and our children's be Thy good pleasure for ever;

    O Lord, our Saviour, we shall never more be moved.

The Lord is worthy to be praised for His judgements with the mouth of His pious ones;

    And blessed be Israel of the Lord for ever.

Psalm IX

The exile of the tribes of Israel. A reference to the covenant which God made with Adam.

When Israel was led away captive into a strange land,

    When they fell away from the Lord who redeemed them,

    They were cast away from the inheritance, which the Lord had given them.

Among every nation were the dispersed of Israel according to the word of God,

    That Thou mightest be justified, O God, in Thy righteousness by reason of our transgressions:

    For Thou art a just judge over all the peoples of the earth.

For from Thy knowledge none that doeth unjustly is hidden,

    And the righteous deeds of Thy pious ones are before Thee, O Lord;

    Where, then, can a man hide himself from Thy knowledge, O God?

Our works are subject to our own choice and power

    To do right or wrong in the works of our hands;

    And in Thy righteousness Thou visitest the sons of men.

He that doeth righteousness layeth up life for himself with the Lord;

    And he that doeth wrongly forfeits his life to destruction;

For the judgements of the Lord are given in righteousness to every man and his house.

Unto whom art Thou good, O God, except to them that call upon the Lord?

> He cleanseth from sins a soul when it maketh confession, when it maketh acknowledgement;

> For shame is upon us and is on our faces on account of all these things.

And to whom doth He forgive sins, except to them that have sinned?

> Thou blessest the righteous, and dost not reprove them for the sins that they have committed;

> And Thy goodness is upon them that sin, when they repent.

And, now, Thou art our God, and we the people whom Thou hast loved:

> Behold and show pity, O God of Israel, for we are Thine;

> And remove not Thy mercy from us, lest they assail us.

For Thou didst choose the seed of Abraham before all the nations,

> And didst set Thy name upon us, O Lord,

> And Thou wilt not reject us for ever.

Thou madest a covenant with our fathers concerning us;

> And we hope in Thee, when our soul turneth unto Thee.

> The mercy of the Lord be upon the house of Israel for ever and ever.

Psalm X

A glorious hymn. Further reference to the eternal covenant between God and Man.

Happy is the man whom the Lord remembereth with reproving,
    And whom He restraineth from the way of evil with strokes
    That he may be cleansed from sin, that it may not be multiplied.
He that maketh ready his back for strokes shall be cleansed,
    For the Lord is good to them that endure chastening.
For He maketh straight the ways of the righteous,
    And doth not pervert them by His chastening.
And the mercy of the Lord is upon them that love Him in truth,
    And the Lord remembereth His servants in mercy.
For the testimony is in the law of the eternal covenant,
    The testimony of the Lord is on the ways of men in His visitation.
Just and kind is our Lord in His judgements for ever,
    And Israel shall praise the name of the Lord in gladness.
And the pious shall give thanks in the assembly of the people;
    And on the poor shall God have mercy in the gladness of Israel;
For good and merciful is God for ever,
    And the assemblies of Israel shall glorify the name of

the Lord.

The salvation of the Lord be upon the house of Israel unto everlasting gladness!

Psalm XI

Jerusalem hears a trumpet and stands on tiptoe to see her children returning from the North, East and West.

Blow ye in Zion on the trumpet to summon the saints,
    Cause ye to be heard in Jerusalem the voice of him that bringeth good tidings;
    For God hath had pity on Israel in visiting them.
Stand on the height, O Jerusalem, and behold thy children,
    From the East and the West, gathered together by the Lord;
From the North they come in the gladness of their God,
    From the isles afar off God hath gathered them.
High mountains hath He abased into a plain for them;
    The hills fled at their entrance.
The woods gave them shelter as they passed by;
    Every sweet-smelling tree God caused to spring up for them,
    That Israel might pass by in the visitation of the glory of their God.
Put on, O Jerusalem, thy glorious garments;
    Make ready thy holy robe;
    For God hath spoken good concerning Israel, for ever and ever.
Let the Lord do what He hath spoken concerning Israel and Jerusalem;
    Let the Lord raise up Israel by His glorious name.

The mercy of the Lord be upon Israel for ever and ever.

Psalm XII

An appeal for family tranquility and peace and quiet at home.

O Lord, deliver my soul from the lawless and wicked man,

From the tongue that is lawless and slanderous, and speaketh lies and deceit.
Manifoldly twisted are the words of the tongue of the wicked man,

Even as among a people a fire that burneth up their beauty.
So he delights to fill houses with a lying tongue,

To cut down the trees of gladness which setteth on fire transgressors,

To involve households in warfare by means of slanderous lips.

May God remove far from the innocent the lips of transgressors by bringing them to want

And may the bones of slanderers be scattered far away from them that fear the Lord!

In flaming fire perish the slanderous tongue far away from the pious!
May the Lord preserve the quiet soul that hateth the unrighteous;

And may the Lord establish the man that followeth peace at home.

The salvation of the Lord be upon Israel His servant for ever;
　　And let the sinners perish together at the presence of
the Lord;
　　But let the Lord's pious ones inherit the promises of the
Lord.

Psalm XIII

Of Solomon. A Psalm. Comfort for the righteous.

The right hand of the Lord hath covered me;
> The right hand of the Lord hath spared us.

The arm of the Lord hath saved us from the sword that passed through,
> From famine and the death of sinners.

Noisome beasts ran upon them:
> With their teeth they tore their flesh,
>
> And with their molars crushed their bones.

But from all these things the Lord delivered us.

The righteous was troubled on account of his errors,
> Lest he should be taken away along with the sinners;

For terrible is the overthrow of the sinner;
> But not one of all these things toucheth the righteous.

For not alike are the chastening of the righteous for sins done in ignorance,
> And the overthrow of the sinners.

Secretly is the righteous chastened,
> Lest the sinner rejoice over the righteous.

For He correcteth the righteous as a beloved son.
> And his chastisement is as that of a first-born.

For the Lord spareth His pious ones,
> And blotteth out their errors by His chastening.

For the life of the righteous shall be for ever;
> But sinners shall be taken away into destruction,

And their memorial shall be found no more.
But upon the pious is the mercy of the Lord,
    And upon them that fear Him His mercy.

Psalm XIV

Sinners "love the brief day spent in companionship with their sin."
Profound wisdom, beautifully expressed.

Faithful is the Lord to them that love Him in truth,
>   To them that endure His chastening,

To them that walk in the righteousness of His commandments,
>   In the law which He commanded us that we might live.

The pious of the Lord shall live by it for ever;
>   The Paradise of the Lord, the trees of life, are His pious ones.

Their planting is rooted for ever;
>   They shall not be plucked up all the days of heaven:

For the portion and the inheritance of God is Israel.
But not so are the sinners and transgressors,
>   Who love the brief day spent in companionship with their sin;
>
>   Their delight is in fleeting corruption,
>
>   And they remember not God.

For the ways of men are known before Him at all times,
>   And He knoweth the secrets of the heart before they come to pass.

Therefore their inheritance is Sheol and darkness and destruction
>   And they shall not be found in the day when the righteous obtain mercy;

But the pious of the Lord shall inherit life in gladness.

Psalm XV

The psalmist restates the great philosophy of Right and Wrong.

When I was in distress I called upon the name of the Lord,
> I hoped for the help of the God of Jacob and was saved;
> For the hope and refuge of the poor art Thou, O God.

For who, O God, is strong except to give thanks unto Thee in truth?
> And wherein is a man powerful except in giving thanks to Thy name?

A new psalm with song in gladness of heart,
> The fruit of the lips with the well-tuned instrument of the tongue,
> The first fruits of the lips from a pious and righteous heart—

He that offereth these things shall never be shaken by evil;
> The flame of fire and the wrath against the unrighteous shall not touch him,

When it goeth forth from the face of the Lord against sinners,
> To destroy all the substance of sinners,

For the mark of God is upon the righteous that they may be saved.
Famine and sword and pestilence shall be far from the righteous,
> For they shall flee away from the pious as men pursued in war;

But they shall pursue sinners and overtake them,

  And they that do lawlessness shall not escape the judgement of God;
As by enemies experienced in war shall they be overtaken,
  For the mark of destruction is upon their forehead.
And the inheritance of sinners is destruction and darkness,
  And their iniquities shall pursue them unto Sheol beneath.
Their inheritance shall not be found of their children,
  For sins shall lay waste the houses of sinners.
And sinners shall perish for ever in the day of the Lord's judgement,
  When God visiteth the earth with His judgement.
But they that fear the Lord shall find mercy therein,
  And shall live by the compassion of their God;
But sinners shall perish for ever.

Psalm XVI

The psalmist again expresses profound truth--"For if Thou givest not strength, who can endure chastisement?"

When my soul slumbered being afar from the Lord, I had all but slipped down to the pit,

    When I was far from God, my soul had been well-nigh poured out unto death,

I had been nigh unto the gates of Sheol with the sinner,

    When my soul departed from the Lord God of Israel--

Had not the Lord helped me with His everlasting mercy.

He pricked me, as a horse is pricked, that I might serve Him,

    My saviour and helper at all times saved me.

I will give thanks unto Thee, O God, for Thou hast helped me to my salvation;

    And hast not counted me with sinners to my destruction.

Remove not Thy mercy from me, O God,

    Nor Thy memorial from my heart until I die.

Rule me, O God, keeping me back from wicked sin,

    And from every wicked woman that causeth the simple to stumble.

And let not the beauty of a lawless woman beguile me,

    Nor any one that is subject to unprofitable sin.

Establish the works of my hands before Thee,

    And preserve my goings in the remembrance of Thee.

Protect my tongue and my lips with words of truth;

Anger and unreasoning wrath put far from me.
Murmuring, and impatience in affliction, remove far from me
When, if I sin, Thou chastenest me that I may return unto Thee.
But with goodwill and cheerfulness support my soul;
When Thou strengthenest my soul, what is given to me will be sufficient for me.
For if Thou givest not strength,
Who can endure chastisement with poverty?
When a man is rebuked by means of his corruption,
Thy testing of him is in his flesh and in the affliction of poverty.
If the righteous endureth in all these trials, he shall receive mercy from the Lord.

Psalm XVII

"They set a worldly monarchy... they lay waste the Throne of David!" A poetic narrative about the utter disintegration of a great nation.

O Lord, Thou art our King for ever and ever,
    For in Thee, O God, doth our soul glory.
How long are the days of man's life upon the earth?
    As are his days, so is the hope set upon him.
But we hope in God, our deliverer;
For the might of our God is for ever with mercy,
    And the kingdom of our God is for ever over the nations in judgement.

Thou, O Lord, didst choose David to be king over Israel,
    And swaredst to him touching his seed that never should his kingdom fail before Thee.
But, for our sins, sinners rose up against us;
    They assailed us and thrust us out;
    What Thou hadst not promised to them, they took away from us with violence.
They in no wise glorified Thy honourable name;
    They set a worldly monarchy in place of that which was their excellency;
    They laid waste the throne of David in tumultuous arrogance.
But Thou, O God, didst cast them down, and remove their seed from the earth,
    In that there rose up against them a man that was alien

to our race.
According to their sins didst Thou recompense them, O God;
    So that it befell them according to their deeds.
God showed them no pity;
    He sought out their seed and let not one of them go free.
Faithful is the Lord in all His judgements
    Which He doeth upon the earth.

The lawless one laid waste our land so that none inhabited it,
    They destroyed young and old and their children together.
In the heat of His anger He sent them away even unto the west,
    And He exposed the rulers of the land unsparingly to derision.
Being an alien the enemy acted proudly,
    And his heart was alien from Our God.
And all things whatsoever he did in Jerusalem,
    As also the nations in the cities to their gods.

And the children of the covenant in the midst of the mingled peoples surpassed them in evil.
    There was not among them one that wrought in the midst of Jerusalem mercy and truth.
They that loved the synagogues of the pious fled from them,
    As sparrows that fly from their nest.
They wandered in deserts that their lives might be saved from harm,

And precious in the eyes of them that lived abroad was any that escaped alive from them.

Over the whole earth were they scattered by lawless men. For the heavens withheld the rain from dropping upon the earth,

Springs were stopped that sprang perennially out of the deeps, that ran down from lofty mountains.

For there was none among them that wrought righteousness and justice;

From the chief of them to the least of them all were sinful;

The king was a transgressor, and the judge disobedient, and the people sinful.

Behold, O Lord, and raise up unto them their king, the son of David,

At the time in the which Thou seest, O God, that he may reign over Israel Thy servant.

And gird him with strength, that he may shatter unrighteous rulers,

And that he may purge Jerusalem from nations that trample her down to destruction.

Wisely, righteously he shall thrust out sinners from the inheritance,

He shall destroy the pride of the sinner as a potter's vessel.

With a rod of iron he shall break in pieces all their substance,

He shall destroy the godless nations with the word of his mouth;

At his rebuke nations shall flee before him,
    And he shall reprove sinners for the thoughts of their heart.
And he shall gather together a holy people, whom he shall lead in righteousness,
    And he shall judge the tribes of the people that has been sanctified by the Lord his God.
And he shall not suffer unrighteousness to lodge any more in their midst,
    Nor shall there dwell with them any man that knoweth wickedness,
    For he shall know them, that they are all sons of their God.
And he shall divide them according to their tribes upon the land,
    And neither sojourner nor alien shall sojourn with them any more.
He shall judge peoples and nations in the wisdom of his righteousness. *Selah.*

And he shall have the heathen nations to serve him under his yoke;
    And he shall glorify the Lord in a place to be seen of all the earth;
    And he shall purge Jerusalem, making it holy as of old:
So that nations shall come from the ends of the earth to see his glory,
    Bringing as gifts her sons who had fainted.

And to see the glory of the Lord, wherewith God hath glorified her.
And he shall be a righteous king, taught of God, over them,
And there shall be no unrighteousness in his days in their midst,
　　For all shall be holy and their king the anointed of the Lord.
For he shall not put his trust in horse and rider and bow,
　　Nor shall he multiply for himself gold and silver for war,
Nor shall he gather confidence from a multitude for the day of battle.
The Lord Himself is his king, the hope of him that is mighty through his hope in God.

All nations shall be in fear before him,
　　For he will smite the earth with the word of his mouth for ever.
He will bless the people of the Lord with wisdom and gladness,
　　And he himself will be pure from sin, so that he may rule a great people.
He will rebuke rulers, and remove sinners by the might of his word;
　　　　And relying upon his God, throughout his days he will not stumble;
For God will make him mighty by means of His holy spirit,
　　And wise by means of the spirit of understanding, with strength and righteousness.

And the blessing of the Lord will be with him: he will be strong and stumble not;

His hope will be in the Lord: who then can prevail against him?

He will, be mighty in his works, and strong in the fear of God,

He will be shepherding the flock of the Lord faithfully and righteously,

And will suffer none among them to stumble in their pasture.

He will lead them all aright,

And there will be no pride among them that any among them should be oppressed.

This will be the majesty of the king of Israel whom God knoweth;

He will raise him up over the house of Israel to correct him.

His words shall be more refined than costly gold, the choicest;

In the assemblies he will judge the peoples, the tribes of the sanctified.

His words shall be like the words of the holy ones in the midst of sanctified peoples.

Blessed be they that shall be in those days,

In that they shall see the good fortune of Israel which God shall bring to pass in the gathering together of the tribes.

May the Lord hasten His mercy upon Israel!

May He deliver us from the uncleanness of unholy enemies!

The Lord Himself is our king for ever and ever.

Psalm XVIII

With this psalm end the warlike Songs of Solomon.

Lord, Thy mercy is over the works of Thy hands for ever;

    Thy goodness is over Israel with a rich gift.

Thine eyes look upon them, so that none of them suffers want;

    Thine ears listen to the hopeful prayer of the poor.

Thy judgements are executed upon the whole earth in mercy;

    And Thy love is toward the seed of Abraham, the children of Israel.

Thy chastisement is upon us as upon a first-born, only-begotten son,

    To turn back the obedient soul from folly that is wrought in ignorance.

May God cleanse Israel against the day of mercy and blessing,

    Against the day of choice when

Blessed shall they be that shall be in those days,

    He bringeth back His anointed.

In that they shall see the goodness of the Lord which He shall perform for the generation that is to come,

Under the rod of chastening of the Lord's anointed in the fear of his God,

    In the spirit of wisdom and righteousness and strength;

That he may direct every man in the works of righteousness by the fear of God,

That he may establish them all before the Lord,
A good generation living in the fear of God in the days of mercy. Selah.
Great is our God and glorious, dwelling in the highest.
It is He who hath established in their courses the lights of heaven for determining seasons from year to year,
And they have not turned aside from the way which He appointed them.
In the fear of God they pursue their path every day,
From the day God created them and for evermore.
And they have erred not since the day He created them.
Since the generations of old they have not withdrawn from their path,
Unless God commanded them so to do by the command of His servants.

www.ingramcontent.com/pod-product-compliance
Lightning Source LLC
LaVergne TN
LVHW041459070426
835507LV00009B/686